A
SNOW SALMON
REACHED
THE
ANDES
LAKE

by Willis Barnstone

CURBSTONE PRESS
AUSTIN • NEW YORK

Certain of these poems have appeared
in the following publications:
*New Letters, Kayak, Yale Review,
Indiana Writes, The Nation.*

Library of Congress Catalog Number 80-65064

ISBN 0-931604-02-8 (cloth)
ISBN 0-931604-03-6 (paper)

Copyright © 1980 by Willis Barnstone

Editors: Ann Sheppard, R. D. Taylor
Design: Margaret Harman
Cover Design: Janet Brooks
Typesetting: G&S Typesetters
Printing: Speleo Press

Printed in the United States of America

Published and Distributed by

Curbstone Press

Box 1613 Main   Box 7445 University Station
New York, N.Y. 10001   Austin, Texas 78712

to Luis Beltrán

Contents

Resolution

A Snow Salmon Reached the Andes Lake

Herons

In the morning
the rain and straw sun sat on the jungle meadows
        and chozas
and swamps where the bulls were belly deep
        in water.
Vultures sat like black teeth in all the plane trees
waiting for a garbage truck to get hauled
        out of the mud.
In the swamp grass around the bulls
and near the naked asses of the dirty children
        of paradise
were the snow herons of peace.

Villa

We two are flying remotely into sleep
and dark
where a young king dozes in exile in his villa.
They bring him honey and chocolate
and sweep the wind from his gate.
Garbage, garbage in the road.
Dont ask me for gardenias; the little girl
        sells them for a peso.
In the dark we sleep under water
between walls of tigerfish
and a young king in his glittering sloop.

Winds on the Tableland

You surprised me. I was sleeping on a bag of sand
        under poplar trees along the Duero river.
I had wandered on the tableland for three years
and never spoke to the peasants in the taverns
or smoked with the February winds
        inhabiting my sleeves.

Then you were there.
The reddish walls of the ancient city were not
        shocked.
The sandtrees and magnolias gave no sign
        to the winter moon.
The merchant threw out the delinquent mother
        and her bony children
while the planet rolled about its pin
        as on an ordinary day.

You came. Surprised the air and painted mountains
        with windy dictionary stars.
The massive news was a secret I smoked each night
        in my room
before the ordinary sun struck the tableland.

Village

Three hawks hang under the harvest moon.
I walk alone at the edge of this ski
      village and worry,
for you who sleep in my ear on the linen hills
are a week away in your house on the rub-a-dub
      mountain.
Is the lamp all night again on fire
      at your smoky desk?

You took me to a high meadow of wind and brown-
            eyed susans,
      time blew among the yellow caraway,
      time filled our tasty science
where a snow salmon reached the Andes lake.
We hiked up to the blue city of big stones,
      lay on stone pastures of the evening,
      lazily threw onions at the Inca stars
and laughed at roman candles. Disappeared.

Three hawks hang over this village where the lamps
      are out. Cold as this slow hour
the peaks are icebergs near the moon.

Travel

An hour before the dawn
I came with a red grip from the north.
In your gown you opened the winter door
     and in half belief we slept
     in half dream our bodies talked
tenderly and with lightning in our thighs
     we soared were fed.
Dawn came deeply in our flesh
and everywhere was dawn, dawn, dawn! The axe
     of time was gone. Rainbow
     of night salmon and sun.
We were fragile and joyful and huge.
     Rainbow.
     We went south
and spoke courteously with Indians and climbed
     together over ancient stones.

Hunting

It is fall
and the Kikuyus are hunting as usual
      on the snow leopard plateaus.
Our captain America finds an oriental solution
      at Songmy
while at home the season is open for death.
Farmers and barbers enter the forest
      of brake and partridge and swamps,
creep like red ants up the Green Mountains,
raise their great phallus to their shoulders
      and pump fire
at the deer of love.
In high Kenya there is fresh snow
while six bulls die in the afternoon in the ring
      of the cheering city of Baeza.

Thrush

The thrush sings behind the woods
and the night blooms with deer.
On the mountain the pumpkins turn slowly
        in red mist.
No one holds up the earth tonight.

I turn out the lamp
and suddenly only you behind the woods
in a port alone in a high reading room
near silver warriors and their jade priest.
Worms hang from trees over a green car
        you take daily like a shower
along the slummy coast.

Our lives are two distant moths burning
        quickly.

Will we hear the thrush sing behind the woods?
hear the sour cherries in the darkness?
see the lake where the four crocodiles
        hold up the corners of the globe?
Will we do the simple things: walk and eat
        and work
and sleep like the moon in its four hundred
        feathers?

The woods scream impatiently.
In their bushes the raspberries turn slowly
        ready to be trampled
and the light blooms with deer.
I am losing myself and you.
I turn out the lamp and run against the evening
        and dont know where to go.

I want to wake.

Dumb

I was angry
and foolish
and stone gray. Dumb as pain.
The clock in the church tower
cleared its lungs
and sang out.
Outside of town I forgot
and saw a yellow deer
spring calmly
through the grass.

Beasts in Patagonia

The page flew over Patagonia.
On its white heart
were the dust and sun of a long day on the table-
    land.
There I roamed after the jade antelope
and tracked the jaguar
into the Land of Fire.
I was a man alone on the continent
yet in my pocket I wore a woman of salt.
The page was a great paper sun
where we read about simple beasts like us.

The Lord is a Woman

Psalm

Whom can I fear when the lord is my light
    and salvation?
And the lord is love.
When I crack or faint I see the lord
    and get up.
When I climb the night tower to seek sleep
    he is the sudden moon
    and I agree to live.
When the sky suffers an earthquake of gray fires
    the drama makes me laugh
    and everyone is funny.
But the lord worries me and I fear for him.
He is more fragile even than I am.
    I must care for him,
    and I question him,
    question the light and salvation.
The lord is a woman, a girl, and they are difficult
    or I am difficult and do not know who
    or if the lord is,
and where, in what gentle wilderness,
    to lose myself.

In Another Solar System

Woman on a planet with a pear sun
when you walk naked in bamboo grass

you are no foolish old saint on earth
or cockroach or silver dog or impostor

dont suffer or die   your schemes are good
and dont be bitter if you love or glance

at a star   listen closely   be happy
here many are morose   live   I'll try too

when you come near our smoky world
I'll leave a light on for you after dark

Cello

Tonight I took the cross and a coke bottle
        and heaved them in the sea
and had to dance very late alone in my room
where the two oil lamps laughed dryly.
Maybe I am learning how to act.

Your face was luminous and happy when you
        surprised me at the door;
you sat on your nightgown and we embraced.
All night the cello played outside and wandered
        on the red rooftops in the Sporades.
By dawn we were so fragile. We were alone
        and danced,
then dressed slowly by the fire of the owls.
Outside, the crane's wing shone in the rose
        of the early sun.
Your face was gone and shone.

Half Moon

Among the hundred cypress trees I walked
    looking for my feet.

Over the marble mountain of Penteli
    came the ship of light,

over shaved heads of tubercular children
    sleeping near their cats.

The half moon glazed like a butcher's lampbulb,
    its dark half was my wonder.

I climbed in its black coffin. There I asked
    for more time near its light.

Chapel

Midnight and observation jeeps parked by the Acheron
        and the unexplored temple
        and prison at Oropos with the composer.
We hear fever in our lungs
and climb carefully on blue mountains
        on the blue ledge over the bay of Euboia
to Saint Peter's small chapel
where we talk and love all night,
a night of milk
and fresh oranges you bring when we are tired.
Our white bird is no dream as it rains
        through the tender dark.
The secret police are sleeping in the room
        beside the royalist officers who failed.
Ferry boats begin to cross the grape morning bay.
You ask my name. It's dawn.

Lions

Even in crazy gloom in the crater of fools
        I lie and daydream
of being that huge torso of Apollo lying cracked
        and serene on the beach
near the palm tree near the gold bridge
        from the ship called Parabola.
I lie
for I see us
hand in hand along the sea urchin shore
        near the plaza of heat and fig trees.

We walk to the torso to the row of canine lions,
        archaic stone pitted with sun,
gazing alive like us at the sea way out.

Way out.
It is a yellow boat. It came and now is lost
        in haze
beyond the Theologian's cave and summit castle
        of monks;
beyond the high chalk village and nothing.
Revelation in the haze.
Through our common cloud of unknowing
        we love and grope
toward a bit of snow we cannot see.

Telephone

All the phones are ripped from those lonely boxes.
    I go down below the street,

fish for a coin and drop my hope in the slot,
    no one home, so I slouch out

and scrawl your name on the subway wall.
    The guard looks at me. No car

to anywhere for now. The ad is dreaming
    rosemary and sage and rye.

Hours hang around the booth. I drop a wreath
    of ivy on the shining tracks.

Rooms Above the Street Below

Open the door, for like a dark woman
sleep lies in my hands.
Through the patio window
forty lions and a lilac tree burn under
     the jasmin moon.
Open the door, for it is dark in the slums
     of New Haven.

I saw the bare hills looming like castanets
and put my razor on the white throat
     of a stray goat.
It is late, love. Forty gray cobras burn
in the snow by the laundromat!
     Open, please. Fix the bed
          so we can sleep.

Squad cars breathe in the cold air below
        like old horses.
The aluminum bars on the delicatessen
are locked and lifeless till morning comes
     to the newspaper machine.
Please come quickly. I'm back from the north
     farm.
After the wind is put outdoors
our black phone will go unused. On it, free,
     we will whisper four kinds of fire.

Wild Iris

In the small scholarly room
where we lived freely between books and lions
        on a mountain of light,
the window over our bed would not shut
        and a winter moon froze on us.
We lay close and kept warm under a Finnish drape.
When you got up to pee or wash
        your soft return was a fawn in the iris
        of a wild brook.
We were distinguished and perfect.

When you typed and typed through the dawn
and I the scholar of one candle
        wrote or dozed,
we meandered freely like the goats in the sun
        in the broken marble reading rooms
        of Asian Pergamon.
Our room froze.   You typed.   I hugged you,
        made you tea and we kept warm.

Lamp

You are naked in the bedroom,
you walk toward the bath,
big and delicate and serene.
Your breasts are a surprise
to the Chinese lamp for they
are full like the ancient song,
your legs are running fawns.
I touch your radiant face.
You walk away handsomer than
the slim moon and more full.

Pension

On the third floor I live near a butler
        and carpenter who play cards
        each long evening in the kitchen
where they chew onions and gossip and leave
        pastry in the sink.
I care for them but they are weak wine
        left in the glass overnight.
Now I must burn our white rooms, clean the grease
        and cinders from the oven,
        hold my breath a while
or gossip with the carpenter about the slumlord
        and the priest.

But you and I in our dry beds
are luckier than the butler and his friend.
In our chaos, in our oven, in our birthday love
        shot down like an outlaw prince,
        I find my way in my head
to find my way to your room by the basso trains
        and Mennonite barn,
and talk to you and comb your hair.

Watersnake and the Orchard

When a watersnake sours the well you are
     alone, your center nowhere.
You shrink on the chalky land of a cemetery
     where bedsheets are underground.
     The night milks and feeds you
with cypresses and jungle birds and a rainbow
     mouth of blood on every fish.

When love is born it is the garden
where you go to hear the pear trees
     and to drink.
There is no end to the sky under the brook.
     To be happy then is out of place.
     You are. Candidly and much more.
     Night is your friend.
When you creep home to your bed you lie
     and shiver in dark light of a sailboat
     crisscrossing the emperor bay of Cape Hatien
     and lobster coves of Maine,
     and come again to the orchard
to hear the pear trees singing of the salt.

When a watersnake sours the well you are
     alone, unlike the sphairos of Empedocles
     (rejoicing in its circular solitude).
Your center is nowhere and your circumference
     everywhere.

Cathedral

When the overhead lights are put out at one,
the library cathedral is dark
but for a few torches in remote meadows.
We wander the gothic halls:
        ghosts
by the padded confession booths with their phones,
through the beehive galleries of the soul
        as Antonio said,
and come in our slow just-we-alone walk
to the great altar where by day the tomes are inked
        and dispensed,
and at last to our firmament—the reading room
        with the Constantine dome
        and million stars carefully shelved.
In the dark (with one match) I steal Virgil for you
        for just a day.
Above us the jeweled ceiling. City of heavenly bodies.

For a brief century we lay our green bags down
        on the night steppes of Asia.
Only the great stone heads on Easter Island
        know where we are.

Stars

We shared the white meat of a coconut
        and slept on the rocky beach
of the bay between the hydroids and the cliffs
looming like great teeth.

(Tell me what I am I said.)

The thistles worked through the blanket
        and tore our ankles.

(You are funny and rich. And your eyes
laugh and taste of coriander.)

Stars came along the evening clouds.
I was a slow ship in you. You cried
and took me like smoke into your lungs,
and starfish at the bottom of your eyes
froze and screamed with light.

(I dont know what you are you said.)
We hear a trumpet piercing the paper sky
        over our three hills.

Night

Often the long night
is an iron mountain
an eyelash of far
firs riding its peak.
I forget a bible
by the tub and climb
outside to see planets
tenting on moon grass.
All over my face
the iron sky explodes.

Pear Tree

Time is running out.
In the spring woods our friends sat and starved
and yesterday they shot themselves.
We still have a week before we die. It is over.
It is past. Time is running out.
On the bus we lay asleep while the fever of the land
was dizzy under the wheels.
If two people become one pear tree in a blue spring
can time murder them
amid the beauty of the sunny morning woods?

Patmos

The dream ends here. Beyond these solitary whales
    and seven stars
we wake. Here is peace. It is not ours.
By steamer we came to the cave of the Revelation
    where a boy is blowing bubblegum
    in the yellow air by the candles.
Is this the end? We lose and we begin, and climb
    nervously. Wind is wild noise.
Sun bakes the white crenelation on the hilltop
    monastery.
The heavens open and a white horse steps
    on mountains in the water.
Can we see? The daystars fall like figs
    cast down by the windmill gale.
The sea is glass mingled with fire.
Fire in us who love. We lose. We wake.
    On the wharf an octopus, in
    each tentacle a horse of salt
    shining like the seven stars.
The dream ends here. Fire in us who lose.
    In the dark cave we see.

White Stockings

I threw a kiss. You disappeared in your VW
        waving.
For eternity?
You drove two hours from village to morning village
        along the ocean to the stony brook
        and lightning played under an oak.
Brutal air hangs over the island.
Are you sleeping under a diamond sheet?

When you disappeared I edged against a fire
        escape. A man in a steaming manhole
        raised his nose and dropped back below.
        I too crawled under the sidewalk;
came up and knew the fruitfly on the night wall
        would not soar.

Yet all this time my feet never lost you.
        You are not gone at all.
        I saw you in a blue chair.
When I turn my foolish back you are sleeping
        in my mouth
and your white stockings laugh.

Walking Trip

Because I cannot climb those steps
rap on the door and call your name

we will not take that walking trip
from Turkey through the eye of Asia

I strip   lie down and try to sleep
at once   it's better not to hear

our deep cello on the night sands
I am a lucky man   you send me

love shining of six yellow tents
I drink hot milk   the spirit rots.

Resolution

Paradise

The old Jew
sat alone

on his bench
in the dark

drawing charts
of the soul.

Daylight fell
on his beard.

He saw flame
he saw flame.

Isaiah

My friend Isaiah was walking in the desolate streets
        of the wasted city.
There was no green thing,
not even waters of destruction and surely no seed
        of a Syrian rose.
No branch of fruit to throw on the sea.

I told the old poet to come up to my room.
We can relax around the kitchen table
and the shadowing wings can fly off beyond the rivers
        of Ethiopia.
He came, took off his coat and helped me again.

Isaiah, you are difficult and great
and walk with flame through the glory of the forest
or climb over thorns into the clouds.
The sky is the flesh of your vision
and I almost faint before your vast indignations.

I am not great. I am a child
so it is still easy to talk to you, a friend.
In me is a forest on a midwest plain.
I hide there
and dont escape, and my sin is that I dont escape.

Cool nights in the forest exhaust me with heat
        of confused longings.
There are no beasts, no devastation, no confounded moor
        nor ashamed sun.
I am a child
and yet I see, see all the time, see light
and so am lost.
Isaiah, have another beer before you leave.

I threw every question at him in the desolate room.
I picked at him and said: This is my soul,
        this is my body. Fix them.
Magnify them.
He spoke of seven stars and one tall nation
and a palace of fishhooks for those who dont leave.

I promised him
I would not see the rain blast the fig trees again,
I promised him
I would not see that light nor the woman in the red dress
        nor the owl on the red tiles.
And while I talked to him I broke my word
and it stank in his nostrils as he went downstairs
        and it was magnified over the roof
while I dreamt again of the light and the red dress
        and did not move.

The Mountain Over the Dead Sea

Snow never burns off the Andes or the glacier
        north of Reykjavik
yet wild herbs I saw at the Masada slope
were dead the next day.
In brown sun I wander the Zealot caves
        above the Roman troops
and swear I'll hold out for years too.
It's delicious to battle or die with faith
        of those zealots and their one God.
My zeal melts. God and the Romans
walked into the Dead Sea, could not come back,
yet I'm happy to burn or starve
lost on the scorched mountain.

Candles

The word is my white room. I live
    alone with her.
She is my child and darkroom sky,
    for with God gone
only the word is a slow parachute
    over the silence
of the vegetable dark. To shape her
    and be shaped by her.
When every year that letter from
    the world informs me
that my nightingales are not for sale,
    I light a candle
and fill the room with paper planes.
    The flaming candle
darkens time. The word can wait.
    Yet since I fail
in love, what if the cock of dawn
    is Christmas dead?
I'm too dumb to know, and keep meddling
    with bits of light.

Rooftop

for my father
d. 1946

You jumped so long ago
now it seems you were
never really here. I know
you were and remember
vaguely. If you could
fly back up to the ledge
and show up today young
as you were, we would go
again out to the desert
or south of green Oaxaca
go on double dates.
We discovered what a window
was the afternoon we chased
bats from our jungle room;
and if I also live close to
the roof, we share a secret
of the good cells on fire
in our black lungs. One night
I failed you. I said no
I could not come. The phone
clicked. You sailed so long
ago out of this world
yet I cant find where
to put that love: the pear
sapling I let wither or
the avocado tree you tore
out of yourself and me.
Our love lay folded neatly
with your coat and felt hat
found on the rooftop
on the day you swan dived
and forgot to sail back up
in the high open sunny air.

Dream

Maybe these poems (which are half my life)
and my life too are not worth more
than guano or Pedro Domec or a few drachma
      or a ton of phosphate. If so,
I would be pleased to leave now
for I am no son of the Buddha
or even of Jesus who came of my dark blood.
I am more a lobster in its pound.
Yet I stay a child with a sly dream
      of waking up,
unafraid of time, released, an orphan free.

Resolution

1

Summer near the cows and taste of blue thorns
with my closest friend (who died that fall).

We talk on two big glacial rocks
        under tasty sun
on our hill high like a grassy moon
over Brandon's white steeples and Mr Ketcham's barn.

I say I will change my life.
No, Larry says, it is not too late.
Birds scream. O but the day is deep with hope.

I dont fear joy but wait too long,
and when the night blows up slowly like an exploding
        bull,
it is clear as pain

and I have changed my life.

2

Winter in this wholly dark bedroom
where I put my glasses on and waddle like a fool
graying
in the dark around the chair clogged with dirty shirts
        for a watch that bounced on the floor.
It has the time.

I resolve there will be time.
I do resolve
as on a summer New England rock
when Mr Ketcham's screaming children in the valley
        seemed like many birds.

This is not the time for truth.

About the Author

Willis Barnstone, poet and critic, is the author of several books of poems, including *From This White Island* (Twayne), *A Day in the Country* (Harper & Row), and *China Poems* (University of Missouri). His anthology *Modern European Poetry* (Bantam) includes major European poets translated by American and British poets. He is also the translator of volumes of poems by Sappho, Saint John of the Cross, Fray Luis de Leon, Pedro Salinas, and Antonio Machado. A Guggenheim Fellow and recipient of both the Cecil Hemley and Lucille Medwick awards from the Poetry Society of America, he is Professor of Comparative Literature at Indiana University.